The Viking Age for Kids

A Captivating Guide to the Vikings, Their Raids, and Everyday Life

© **Copyright 2023 - All rights reserved.**

The content contained within this book may not be reproduced, duplicated, or transmitted without direct written permission from the author or the publisher.

Under no circumstances will any blame or legal responsibility be held against the publisher, or author, for any damages, reparation, or monetary loss due to the information contained within this book, either directly or indirectly.

Legal Notice:

This book is copyright protected. It is only for personal use. You cannot amend, distribute, sell, use, quote, or paraphrase any part, or the content within this book, without the consent of the author or publisher.

Disclaimer Notice:

Please note the information contained within this document is for educational and entertainment purposes only. All effort has been executed to present accurate, up-to-date, reliable, and complete information. No warranties of any kind are declared or implied. Readers acknowledge that the author is not engaging in the rendering of legal, financial, medical, or professional advice. The content within this book has been derived from various sources. Please consult a licensed professional before attempting any techniques outlined in this book.

By reading this document, the reader agrees that under no circumstances is the author responsible for any losses, direct or indirect, that are incurred as a result of the use of the information contained within this document, including, but not limited to, errors, omissions, or inaccuracies.

Table of Contents

Introduction 1
Chapter 1: Who Were the Vikings? 2
Chapter 2: Ships and Raids 9
Chapter 3: Trade and Tribute 14
Chapter 4: Daily Viking life and Society 19
Chapter 5: The Viking Sagas 27
Chapter 6: Religion: Gods and Goddesses 34
Chapter 7: Tales of Norse Mythology 42
Chapter 8: Runes and Rituals 51
Chapter 9: What Happened to the Vikings? 58
Chapter 10: Fun Viking Facts 63
If you want to learn more about tons of other exciting historical periods, check out our other books! 70
Bibliography 72

INTRODUCTION

Have you ever wondered how much of what you know about Vikings is real and how much is fantasy? Were they really as fearsome and terrifying as history books and TV would have us believe? What was ordinary life like for a Viking? Why did the Viking Age start? Why did the Vikings disappear? All of these questions and more will be answered in this book.

Uncover more about who the Vikings were, from their history to notable figures and what their daily lives were like. You'll also learn more about their beliefs. So, let's dive in and explore the Viking Age and the legacies these notorious warrior people left behind.

Be sure to have a go at the fun activities at the end of each chapter to enjoy the full Captivating History experience!

Chapter 1: Who Were the Vikings?

The Vikings were a group of people who lived in northern Europe in medieval times. To start with, they were in *Scandinavia* (Sweden, Norway, and Denmark). The Viking Age took place from 793 to 1066 CE.

The Vikings were fierce warriors. They would go on raiding expeditions in longships to other nearby countries. The Vikings were almost like pirates. They enjoyed sailing the seas. They also plundered and burned villages. Vikings often killed people during their raids. Although the Vikings are referred to as one group, they were actually made up of several tribes and clans.

A picture showing Viking warriors on a boat going raiding.
Becherel, CC BY-SA 3.0 <https://creativecommons.org/licenses/by-sa/3.0>, via Wikimedia Commons, https://commons.wikimedia.org/w/index.php?curid=18154876

Vikings were also called *Norsemen* or Northmen because they came from the north. The word "Viking" actually means "to raid" or "piracy" in Old Norse (the language they spoke). The Vikings did not call themselves this. After all, the word "Viking" was used to describe what they were doing! Instead, they would say they are "going on a Viking."

Not all Norsemen were Vikings. But most Europeans only had contact with Vikings through their raids. This is why Vikings and Norsemen are often used interchangeably.

Fun Fact: "Vik" in Old Norse means "harbor."

The Viking Era began in 793 CE when the Vikings first raided England and the holy island of *Lindisfarne (lin-duh-sfaan)*. The Vikings quickly gained a bad reputation among the English. It was hard not to see the Vikings in a bad light. They would raid defenseless monasteries where monks lived. Monks were religious men of the Catholic Church who lived a life of *solitude* (isolation) and devotion to God. They were very respected during the Middle Ages.

Monasteries had no weapons or defenses against attacks. The Vikings saw the monasteries as easy targets. They would take their gold and even capture monks to sell as slaves. The Vikings were branded as barbarians because of their cruel raids and lack of respect for Christianity.

The Vikings also formed settlements in other countries. In the 9th century, they began to settle in Britain, Iceland, and Germany. They also gained control of the Northern Isles off Scotland and founded several trading towns in Ireland. The Vikings gained control of northern England in 851 CE until they were finally forced out in 952 CE.

In 865 CE, *the Great Heathen Army* arrived in England. The army was led by the sons of *Ragnar Lothbrok (rang-nah loth-brewk)*. He was a legendary Viking king who led many raids. Lothbrok's son, *Ivan the Boneless*, led an army of four thousand men to attack England. The raids lasted for fourteen years. Eventually, the *Anglo-Saxons* (the people living in England) paid them a ransom in gold and silver to stop.

Fun Fact: Ragnar Lothbrok was said to have been killed by being thrown into a pit of snakes.

Another famous Viking raid was the capture of York, England. This happened on November 1st, 866 CE. The Vikings might have chosen this date because it was All Saints Day. The people of York were busy attending church and celebrating the festival. The Vikings were able to catch them by surprise.

By 866 CE, the Danish Vikings had colonized much of northern and eastern England. The *Danelaw* (Danish law) was established in these areas. The king of *Wessex* (a former kingdom in England) agreed with the Danelaw to maintain peace.

England wasn't the only country the Vikings invaded. In 845 CE, the Vikings *besieged* (surrounded) Paris, France. Over one hundred longships attacked. The Vikings easily defeated the French army. However, they left after the king gave them gold and silver.

In the 10th century, the Vikings expanded into the northeastern parts of Europe and Russia. They also moved into France again. This time, they established Normandy. Normandy would go on to play an important role in French politics.

Fun Fact: Normandy means "Northmen" in Old Norse.

A map of the Viking raids and settlements.
https://commons.wikimedia.org/w/index.php?curid=2299978

By the start of the 11th century, the Vikings had reached their peak. One Viking even went as far as North America. He formed a settlement in what is now Canada. This was almost five hundred years before the Americas were "discovered" by Christopher Columbus!

Leif Erikson (leef-eh-ruhk-sn) discovered North America. He was from Greenland. He set off in 1000 CE to search for a land that had been spotted by another Viking whose ship was blown off course on the way to Greenland. Leif returned home with valuable timber from Canada. He never returned to America, but other Vikings followed in his footsteps. However, the Vikings did not remain in Canada long. They might have been forced out by the natives.

Fun Fact: Leif Erikson's father, Erik Thorvaldsson (thor-val-son) (nicknamed Erik the Red for his red hair), formed the first Viking settlement in Greenland. He discovered it after he had been banished from Norway and Iceland for killing people.

A painting called Leif Erikson discovers America.
https://commons.wikimedia.org/w/index.php?curid=91487736

Fun Fact: In 1013 CE, England was ruled by a Viking king named Sweyn (sven) Forkbeard. His rule only lasted five weeks before he died.

The end of the Viking Age is generally regarded to be 1066 CE. The last great Viking king, *King Harald Hardrada* of Norway, was one of three men who believed he was the rightful heir to the throne of England. He led his army in a battle against the Anglo-Saxons. Even though he had the fearsome Vikings on his side, he was defeated. *Duke William of Normandy*, commonly known as *William the Conqueror*, became the king of England after winning the Battle of Hastings that same year.

We'll find out a bit more about what happened to the Vikings in Chapter 9!

Chapter 1 Challenge Activity

Can you find the following words in this word search?

Barbarian, Viking, Old Norse, Norsemen, Raid, Monk, Monastery, Longship

V	I	K	I	N	G	L	L	V
M	L	B	K	A	U	O	O	I
O	P	A	L	M	O	N	O	E
N	Z	R	H	G	Y	G	L	H
A	F	B	R	S	E	S	D	K
S	O	A	W	I	V	H	N	G
T	A	R	A	I	D	I	O	S
E	B	I	P	C	B	P	R	T
R	T	A	L	J	T	S	S	A
Y	Q	N	O	R	S	E	E	N

Chapter 1 Answer

Can you find the following words in this word search?

Barbarian, Viking, Old Norse, Norsemen, Raid, Monk, Monastery, Longship

V	I	K	I	N	G	L	L	V
M	L	B	K	A	U	O	O	I
O	P	A	L	M	O	N	O	E
N	Z	R	H	G	Y	G	L	H
A	F	B	R	S	E	S	D	K
S	O	A	W	I	V	H	N	G
T	A	R	A	I	D	I	O	S
E	B	I	P	C	B	P	R	T
R	T	A	L	J	T	S	S	A
Y	Q	N	O	R	S	E	E	N

Chapter 2: Ships and Raids

The Vikings couldn't have raided and settled in so many countries without their ships. Viking ships, known as *longships*, were longer than most boats. They ranged between forty-five to seventy-five feet long. They were made of timber (usually oak). The longships made it easier for the Vikings to travel farther distances and handle rough seas.

There were benches and *oars* (long wooden sticks with flat-bladed ends used to propel the boats forward) inside the longships. Between forty to sixty *oarsmen* would be needed. Longships often had shields positioned along the sides. Longships had a single *mast* (the tall post that the sail was attached to) and a square *sail* (a piece of material attached to the mast that would catch the wind, moving the boat forward).

Longships also had a *keel*. A keel is the main base of the ship. It runs along the center of the boat. The *hull* (the main body of the ship) is attached to the keel. The longships had pointed ends, allowing the boat to go forward or backward without needing to turn around. Perhaps the most iconic feature of Viking longships was their curved *prows* (the portion of the ship that sticks out above the water).

Fun Fact: Longships were built using the "clinker" method. Planks of timber were overlapped and nailed together. Then the ship was made watertight by filling any gaps in the planks with tarred animal hair.

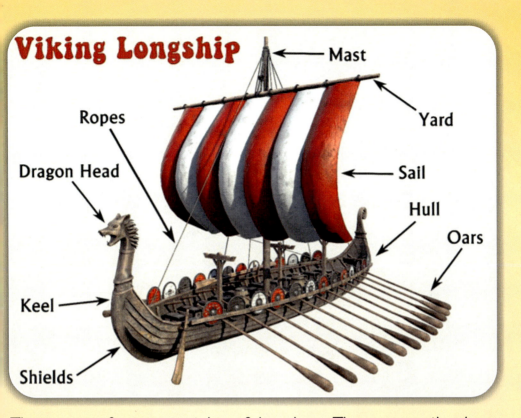

There were four main styles of longships. There were the *karvi* (kar-vay), *snekkja* (snekke), *skeid* (side), and *drakkar* (dreki). Karvi ships were the smallest. They would have six to sixteen rowing benches. Although they were used in war, they were primarily used for trading, transportation, and fishing. Because of their smaller size, they were better suited to handle shallow waters.

Perhaps you've guessed already what snekkja might mean. Snekkja means "snake." The ships were given this nickname because of their long and sleek style. The snekkja ships were perfect for battles and raids. They were excellent at handling rough, open seas. On average, they were around fifty-six feet long. They could carry around forty oarsmen.

Snekkjas had gently curved hulls so they could land on beaches. They were great for Atlantic expeditions and traveling the many fjords (fyords) found in Norway and Greenland. (Fjords are long narrow stretches of water with steep cliffs around the sides created by glaciers.)

Fun Fact: The Sognefjord (song-nuh-fyord) is almost one hundred miles long. It is the biggest and deepest fjord in Norway.

Skeid longships were the largest longships. Its name translates to "slider." They were primarily used for warfare. They could carry more men thanks to their bigger size. One of the biggest skeids ever discovered was 121 feet long!

We know the least about the drakkar, which means "dragon." The prows often had carvings of dragons. So, the boats were nicknamed "dragon ships." They also had other carvings on them, like snakes.

A replica of a Viking longship, Hugin, in Ramsgate, Kent, England.
By Peter Lelliott, CC BY-SA 2.0, https://creativecommons.org/licenses/by-sa/2.0/deed.en, https://commons.wikimedia.org/w/index.php?curid=8380556

The carvings were said to serve two purposes. They warded off evil sea spirits and monsters. They also intimidated the villages the Vikings were about to raid since they looked like giant monsters emerging from the sea.

We know the Vikings used their longships to go on raids. But why did the Vikings go raiding? The primary reason was for gold and slaves. The Vikings would bring their loot home to sell. Later on, the Vikings decided to settle in the lands they raided instead of simply taking things home.

The Vikings relied on the element of surprise. They often arrived in the early hours of the morning while many people were still sleeping. They overwhelmed the sleeping villages, quickly stealing all their valuables and kidnapping slaves before getting back in their boats and leaving.

The longships were an important part of how Vikings were able to take people by surprise. They were able to bring their ships right up onshore to arrive and leave as quickly as possible.

Chapter 2 Challenge Activity

Draw your own Viking ship. Be sure to include the important elements, such as a mast, sail, hull, keel, shields, oars, and prows!

Chapter 3: Trade and Tribute

Vikings didn't just raid and plunder the countries they visited. They also traded with them. But why would they steal from some and trade with others? Well, it's fairly simple. The Vikings raided places that were poorly defended. They could easily defeat them and take their goods. But when they came across better-defended towns, they chose to trade with them instead.

The Vikings in Norway and Denmark commonly traveled west to France, Britain, and Scotland. The Swedish Vikings went east toward Russia and even as far south as *Constantinople* (modern-day Istanbul, Turkey). Some Viking merchants traveled even farther east into Iraq, and some even made it as far west as the Americas.

In the west, they traded animal skins and furs, walrus tusks, amber, and iron. Settlers also created crafts like dishes, pottery, leather goods, cloth, and jewelry. Blacksmiths made weapons and armor. They would trade these goods and slaves captured in raids. In the east, the Vikings traded slaves and other goods in exchange for spices, silks, fruit, and wine.

When traveling, the Vikings tried to stay as close to the coastline as possible. By doing this, they could see landmarks, which helped to guide them. If this was not possible, they used the sun to point them in the right direction. The Vikings invented a type of sundial that helped point the way by using shadows from the sun.

At night, they would look at the stars to map their course. Viking sailors were so experienced that they could tell when land was near based on the color of the water or by watching birds.

In the beginning, the Vikings bartered with other cities. Later on, they paid for goods instead. Their newfound wealth came from raids, trade, and *tribute* (goods that countries paid the Vikings in exchange for peace).

> **Fun Fact:** Vikings carried a set of folding scales to measure the weight of coins. They wanted to make sure they were getting paid correctly and got the best deal.

Viking coin weights.
EttuBruta, CC BY-SA 4.0 <https://creativecommons.org/licenses/by-sa/4.0>, via Wikimedia Commons, https://commons.wikimedia.org/w/index.php?curid=48909424

Some countries, like England and France, introduced taxes known as a *Danegeld*. The Danegeld could be used as a way to pay off the Vikings to avoid an attack. It could also be used as a *stipend (sty-pend)*. Sometimes, other countries paid the Vikings in exchange for their services as warriors.

The tributes were not popular with the people since they made them even poorer. They resented giving the barbarian invaders any more money than they had already taken. Tributes also didn't work very well. Eventually, the Vikings would come back and demand more.

Because of their fearsome reputation as warriors, the Vikings were often hired to fight for different countries. For example, they were hired to fight for the *Varangian (vr-an-jee-uhn) Guard*, an elite unit of the *Byzantine* army. The Byzantine Empire's capital was Constantinople. The Varangian Guard served as bodyguards for the Byzantine emperors. The Vikings were ideal guards.

Calling of the Varangian Guard by A. Krivshenko (1889).
https://commons.wikimedia.org/w/index.php?curid=55667540

Sometimes, the Vikings had to offer something other than their goods or skills if they wanted something more than money. We can find an example of this in the story of *Rollo of Normandy*. Rollo was a Viking chief who became the founder of Normandy. But for him to be able to achieve this, he first had to make a deal with the king of France, *Charles the Simple*. In exchange for the land, Rollo agreed to convert to Christianity. He also promised to protect the region from any new Viking invaders. He promised to restore order and marry Charles's daughter, *Gisla*.

Fun Fact: Another part of Rollo's deal with the king was that he had to change his name to Robert!

Christian writers would later describe Rollo very favorably. They saw him as a savage Viking who saw the error of his ways and embraced God. Whether or not this was the case, Rollo kept his promise. He also introduced Viking laws based on honor. Vikings believed in taking responsibility for one's actions.

Fun Fact: Rollo was the great-great-great grandfather of William the Conqueror, the first Norman king of England!

A statue of Rollo depicted among the six dukes of Normandy in the town square of Falaise.

Imars: Michael Shea., CC BY-SA 2.5 <https://creativecommons.org/licenses/by-sa/2.5>, via Wikimedia Commons, https://commons.wikimedia.org/w/index.php?curid=9553228

Chapter 3 Challenge Activity

Imagine you are a Viking or a merchant in a faraway land. Draw a poster advertising your goods for the Vikings or merchants with whom you might wish to trade. What types of items would you sell that might be appealing to a Viking? Or what kind of goods or services do you have to offer as a Viking? Make it as colorful and creative as you like. Include lots of drawings and descriptions!

Chapter 4: Daily Viking Life and Society

Although we often think of Vikings as fierce warriors and explorers, this wasn't the case. Most Vikings were farmers. They grew crops like oats, barley, and rye. They also tended to livestock. Their farms had sheep, goats, pigs, cows, horses, and chickens. Everyone helped on the farm, but men and women had different responsibilities.

Women's tasks centered around the home. They made clothing and ran the household. They prepared and cooked food. They were also responsible for milking the cows and goats. The women used the milk to make other dairy products like cream, cheese, and butter.

Fun Fact: Butter has existed since 8000 BCE. In 600 CE, the butter churn became popular in Europe.

A drawing of a butter churn.
Лобачев Владимир, CC BY-SA 4.0 <https://creativecommons.org/licenses/by-sa/4.0>, via Wikimedia Commons, https://commons.wikimedia.org/w/index.php?curid=95481610

Viking men only went on raids if they weren't farming. They were responsible for the more labor-intensive work on the farm. They plowed, planted seeds, and harvested the crops. They left the most disgusting and difficult tasks to their slaves. This included building, pulling the plows, and spreading the dung. Pee-ew!

Many Vikings were fishermen or merchants because lots of Viking towns were on the coast. Salt was a valuable resource that merchants traded. Salt could be used to preserve fish and meat during the winter when food was scarce.

Fun Fact: Viking fishermen even hunted whales!

There were other jobs available too. Craftsmen made shoes, belts, and silverware. Potters made clay pots for cooking and storing food and drinks. Blacksmiths made horseshoes, weapons, and armor. They also forged metal tools for farming, cooking, and hunting. There were even jewelers. They made brooches, rings, and necklaces.

One of the most important jobs for a Viking was building longships! A master shipbuilder called a *hofudsmidir (ho-fuhds-midr)* led the boat builders, or *filungar (fi-lunh-ga)*. The hofudsmidir was responsible for paying the workers and getting the materials to build the longship.

At the very top of Viking society were chiefs. They ruled the tribe. Below them were *jarls*. Jarls were wealthy traders and landowners. The biggest group was the *karls*. Karls were craftsmen and farmers. At the bottom of the hierarchy were *thralls*. Thralls were slaves captured during raids. They had to do the worst jobs. They could be severely punished or killed if they tried to escape. A thrall could buy their freedom if they made enough money.

Viking clothing was simple and practical. Clothes were made from wool and linen. Shoes were made from leather. Animal furs were worn in the winter. Men wore loose-fitting pants and tunics. Women wore loose apron dresses known as *hangerock* or *smokkr*. Vikings wore jewelry and decorative brooches that fastened cloaks.

Reconstructed Viking costumes on display at the Museum of Archaeology in Stavanger, Norway. The woman is wearing a white underdress, a red hangerock or smokkr, and brooches.
Wolfmann, CC BY-SA 4.0 <https://creativecommons.org/licenses/by-sa/4.0>, via Wikimedia Commons, https://commons.wikimedia.org/w/index.php?curid=40572419

Viking houses were built from timber and had thatched roofs made of reeds or straw. Their homes were long and rectangular. They usually only had one big room. There were no windows or chimneys. There was one opening for the smoke from the fire. This meant the houses were very dark and smokey.

There wasn't much furniture inside the home. Wooden benches doubled as seats and beds. Only wealthy families had tables. Animal furs were draped over the floor, benches, and even the walls to make the homes warmer and cozier. There was no bathroom inside the house. Instead, the Vikings would use a *cesspit* (a hole dug into the ground) outside.

If the family wasn't rich enough to build a barn, the animals would sleep inside the house at night! Although this was very smelly, it provided some much-needed extra warmth in the winter months!

Reconstruction of Viking houses.
Frank Vincentz, CC BY-SA 3.0 <https://creativecommons.org/licenses/by-sa/3.0>,
via Wikimedia Commons, https://commons.wikimedia.org/w/index.php?curid=28299550

While it might sound like Viking homes were dirty and smelly, the Vikings were actually obsessed with being clean. They swept and cleaned the house regularly. They bathed at least once a week. That was a lot in those days! Vikings also brushed their hair often. The Vikings were always clean and well-groomed because they believed that when they died, they would appear before the gods exactly as they had died. They didn't want to be dirty or smelly in front of the gods!

Fun Fact: Vikings even ironed their clothes using hot stones.

Viking children didn't go to school. They were taught skills by their parents. Boys learned to farm and raid. Girls learned how to take care of the home. Children helped out at a young age. They prepared food and built fires. They might gather firewood, fruits, and berries. Children also would help tend to the animals.

It wasn't all work for Viking children. They played games too. They played with dolls, ships, and swords made from wood.

Life was very difficult during the Viking Age. The average life expectancy was between forty to forty-five years old. It was not uncommon for a bad harvest to cause famine. Diseases easily spread. An estimated 30 to 40 percent of Viking children never made it to adulthood. If a family was very poor and couldn't afford to feed another child, the family might leave the baby outside to die. This also happened when the baby was born with problems and unlikely to survive. This practice was outlawed once the Vikings adopted Christianity.

Although life was hard for the Vikings, they still found time to have fun. They enjoyed playing games to test each other's strength and agility. They gathered for celebrations and events, where they enjoyed music and sports. Another popular Viking activity was sitting around the fire at night and telling stories. These stories were usually about the Norse gods.

Faroe stamps depicting everyday life in the Viking Age.
https://commons.wikimedia.org/w/index.php?curid=378398

Chapter 4 Activity

Pick one (or both) of the fun and creative activities below to complete!

A. Build your own Viking house!

   We recommend using a cardboard box for the building and string, rope, or something similar to make the thatched roof. Then design the inside! Make or draw animals, a fireplace, wooden benches, furs, or even a Viking family and games! There's no limit to what you can make, so get creative!

B. Make homemade butter!

   Have a go at making your very own handmade butter at home! (The handmade method in a jar is a bit trickier, but it is fun and gives you a better understanding of how difficult and time-consuming it was for the Viking women!)

All you'll need are the following ingredients/items:

- 1 cup of heavy whipping cream
- A large bowl of ice water
- Salt to taste (optional)
- A mixer, blender, or mason jar with a tight-fitting lid
- A sieve or cheesecloth

Method

Mixer/blender (Be sure to get an adult to help with this step!)

1. Pour in the cream. Beat at a low speed. Gradually increase the speed as the mixture thickens.
2. After several minutes, whipped cream will form. Keep mixing. It will start to turn yellow. After several more minutes, the fat will start to separate from the liquid, and clumps of butter will begin to form.
3. Strain the solid butterfat clumps from the buttermilk using a sieve or cheesecloth. (You can save the buttermilk for another recipe if you want!)
4. Pour cold water over the butter. Repeat with new water two more times.

5. Shape the butter into whatever shape you like. You can now add any salt, spices, or herbs that you like, or you can enjoy it as it is!

Mason Jar

1. Pour the cream into the jar, filling it only halfway. (Be sure not to overfill more than halfway, or it won't work!) Screw the lid on nice and tight so nothing leaks out.
2. Shake the jar vigorously for around 5 to 7 minutes. After a few minutes, whipped cream will form. Keep shaking until a lump forms inside. Then shake for another minute. You should now see that the fat solids have separated from the liquid. This can take longer. It depends on how vigorously you shake!
3. Strain the solid butterfat clumps from the buttermilk using a sieve or cheesecloth. (You can save the buttermilk for another recipe if you want!)
4. Pour cold water over the butter. Repeat with new water two more times.

    Shape the butter into whatever shape you like. You can now add any salt, spices, or herbs that you like, or you can enjoy it as it is!

Chapter 5: The Viking Sagas

Sagas (saa-guhs) are Norse legends and historical stories. Most sagas are recognizable and have similar traits. They were originally passed down orally. As you now know, the Vikings liked to sit around and tell stories. The sagas mostly come from Iceland. They were written in the 12th to 15th centuries.

The sagas are all written in Old Norse. Most of the authors are *anonymous* (the writers didn't include their names). The stories tend to be told *chronologically* (in order of when they happened). They also focused on everyday life. It is often confusing to know what is true and what is fiction in the sagas. The legends and historical facts are often mixed together.

Fun Fact: It is thought the sagas were performed or read aloud for entertainment.

A page from an Icelandic manuscript.
https://commons.wikimedia.org/w/index.php?curid=21714684

The Norse sagas can be divided roughly into five different genres:

1. Legendary sagas featuring the gods and mythical monsters.
2. Sagas about kings.
3. Sagas about knights.
4. Family sagas or stories about Viking families.
5. Contemporary sagas. These focused on people who were alive when the writer of the saga was alive. Usually, these sagas would be about powerful families.

The sagas featured normal people and their lives. They also described epic adventures. The sagas talked about the Viking raids. One saga told of Erik the Red and his son Leif's discovery of the Americas. Others were about the gods and their exploits.

Like ancient Greek mythology, the Norse sagas had lots of different mythical creatures. There were giants (storm, rock, and ice ones), sea snakes, lava monsters, dragons, and more. Let's learn more about some of the creatures you might find in a saga.

The Kraken

You may have already heard of the *Kraken (kra-kin)*. It is still featured in films, TV, and books today! The Kraken was the most fearsome monster of all. It was a giant octopus-like creature that lived in the sea. It would drag ships down to the bottom of the ocean. Once the Kraken grabbed ahold of your boat, your only chance of survival was to jump overboard and hope for rescue!

The Kraken wasn't just a Viking monster. It was in folklore from other countries too!

> **Fun Fact:** It is thought the legend of the Kraken might have come from a sighting of a giant squid! Giant squid can grow to between forty and fifty feet!

The Mare

This monster is one of the reasons we call bad dreams nightmares! The Mare would sit on a person at night and give them bad dreams. The Vikings thought it wouldn't harm them if they couldn't see it.

The Fossegrim

This ghost haunted creeks and brooks while playing a fiddle. The Vikings knew the *Fossegrim (fossy-grym)* was near if they heard its fiddle and running water. They weren't sure if it was dangerous or not, but they avoided it just in case!

The Nokken

The *Nokken (nuh-ken)* was a shapeshifter who lived in ponds. It could assume any shape. It could appear as a handsome young man and lure beautiful women to their deaths by drowning. It couldn't be out of the water for long. When it was, it would appear as a white horse and try to tempt children to ride it to their doom. The Nokken could also pretend to be a wooden boat. It would drag you under if you went in the water to get the boat.

The Vikings had lots of tricks to protect themselves against the Nokken. One way to stop it was by saying its name three times. Vikings carried special amulets and charms to keep the Nokken away. They thought that if you threw a piece of metal into the water while it was attacking, it would save them. So, most Vikings always had some metal on them just to be safe!

Nokken by Theodor Kittelsen, 1887-92.
https://commons.wikimedia.org/w/index.php?curid=225207

The Pesta

The legendary *Pesta (pes-ta)* came about because of the *bubonic (bew-boh-nick) plague* (also known as the Black Death). The plague spread throughout Europe in the Middle Ages. It was deadly and killed millions of people in just a few years. People didn't know what caused it. The Vikings believed Pesta was to blame. Pesta appeared as an old woman wearing all black. She carried a broom and a rake. If you saw Pesta, you would catch the plague and die. Many brave Vikings tried to kill Pesta if they saw her. They wanted to save their families.

Fun Fact: Because of this legend, Viking women wore bright colors so they wouldn't be mistaken for Pesta!

Nisses

Nisses (nee-suhs) were a type of goblin. Every Viking home had at least one nisse living in their barn. Nisses protected the animals and home in exchange for gifts. People would leave the nisses things like tiny hats and clothes, turned-up-toed shoes, and little toys or food. You could try to become friends with a nisse by giving it gifts. If it liked you, you might catch a glimpse of it.

Nisses were very old. They had long, white beards and red hats. They looked like garden gnomes.

Nisses loved to play pranks on people. But at Christmastime, they would do something very nice. They would sneak into the home and leave presents for the children in their shoes or stockings!

Trolls

According to Vikings, trolls were very mean and very stupid. They could be big or small. Every mountain range had trolls inside. Each troll tribe had a king. Troll kings were the biggest of them all. They had many heads but only one eye. Troll kings were very dirty, which made their many heads itchy! The king commanded the other trolls to kidnap Viking maidens to come and scratch his heads. He needed one woman per head. The troll queen only had one head, but she could remove it and carry it around!

Not all trolls lived in the mountains. Some lived under bridges, but they weren't much nicer!

A drawing of a troll becoming a mountain.
illustator: JNL - Own work, FAL, https://commons.wikimedia.org/w/index.php?curid=385366

The Icelandic people are very proud of their sagas. They still tell them today. Many Icelanders claim to be distant relatives of the heroes in the stories. Given how few people live in Iceland today (only 320,000 people), it's possible they are! Many modern books, movies, and TV shows have been influenced by sagas.

In our next chapter, you'll learn about the Viking gods and goddesses. You might be amazed at how many of them you already know and love! (Hint: you might know one of them as a hammer-wielding superhero!)

Chapter 5 Activity

Write an epic saga. Write a story with you (or anyone else you'd like) as the hero! Try to include one or more of the creatures you learned about in this chapter. Like any true saga, don't forget to include details of daily life and the hero's achievements!

Chapter 6: Religion: Gods and Goddesses

The Vikings originally believed in the Old Norse gods and goddesses. Old Norse was a *polytheistic (po-lee-thee-i-stuhk)* religion. This meant they believed in more than one god. The worship of the Old Norse gods is called *asatro (a-suh-tro)*. However, this is a new term. The Vikings did not have a name for their religion. Instead, they referred to it as "the old way." They called Christianity "the new way."

The Vikings also worshiped their ancestors and giants. Although many Vikings converted to Christianity, not all of them completely gave up their beliefs. Many continued to practice in secret.

Fun Fact: Today, approximately five hundred to one thousand people in Denmark still believe in the Old Norse gods. Other believers of asatro are in Sweden, Norway, Iceland, the United Kingdom, and the United States.

The Vikings had many different gods. Each played a different role. Many of them are now famous thanks to the popular Marvel movies. How many do you know?

Odin

Odin (oh-din) was the king of the gods and the god of war. He was also the god of wisdom, healing, and death. Odin was described as a bearded older man. He had one eye and wore a cloak and a hat. Odin was also often shown riding a horse with eight legs called *Sleipnir (slayp-neer)*. He was also accompanied by two wolves, *Geri (jerry)* and *Freki (frey-kee)*.

Odin had two ravens named *Huginn (hoo-gn)* and *Muninn (moo-nuhn)*. They flew around the world and reported what they saw to him.

Odin was the most revered of the Norse gods. He caused battles on earth by throwing his magical spear, *Gungnir (ghun-neer)*.

A drawing of Odin on his throne.
https://commons.wikimedia.org/w/index.php?curid=5251205

Frigg

Frigg (frig) was Odin's wife. Frigg was a loyal and devoted wife to Odin, even though he wasn't always a good husband to her. Frigg was also the goddess of the sky, marriage, fertility, family, and wisdom.

Thor

Thor was Odin's son and the god of thunder and lightning. Thor's weapon, *Mjölnir (me-yol-neer)*, was a powerful hammer. It was capable of killing giants and smashing mountains. When Thor threw his hammer, it created lightning. The wheels of his chariot made the sounds of thunder. Two giant goats pulled Thor's chariot.

Thor was the strongest god and the people's favorite. Given his popularity in the Marvel movies, we'd say he's still the people's favorite!

Fun Fact: Viking men wore charms of Thor's hammer around their necks for good luck.

A painting of Thor fighting giants.
https://commons.wikimedia.org/w/index.php?curid=22007120

Loki

Loki (low-kee) was a trickster god of mischief. He was able to shapeshift into different forms. He would both help and hinder the gods. Loki wasn't evil, but his mischievous nature could cause a lot of harm.

Balder

Balder (baal-der) was the son of Odin and Frigg. He was the god of light and purity. Balder was the most handsome of the gods. He was good, kind, and fair.

Although he was immortal, there was a prophecy predicting his death. To try and prevent this, Frigg consulted every entity in the cosmos. She made them swear they wouldn't harm him. But Frigg didn't ask the mistletoe. She believed it was small and harmless. When Loki heard of this, he made an arrow from mistletoe. The arrow was accidentally fired at Balder, killing him.

Hel

Hel was the goddess of *Helheim (hell-haaim)*, the Viking underworld. Hel was Loki's daughter. The entrance of Helheim was guarded by her ferocious pet, *Garmr (gah-mur)*, a giant wolf/dog.

Fun Fact: Hel's bottom half was a skeleton!

Freya

Freya was the goddess of love, beauty, gold, war, fate, and fertility. She wore a cloak made from falcon feathers. She would also cry tears of gold. Two cats pulled Freya's chariot. She also rode her pet boar, *Hildisvíni (hill-diss-vee-nee)*.

A painting of Freya and Odin.
https://commons.wikimedia.org/w/index.php?curid=5220642

Frey

Frey was Freya's twin brother. He was the god of farming, fertility, the sun, and the rain. Viking farmers painted a picture of Frey on their wagons in the hopes of having a successful harvest.

The home of the gods was *Asgard (as-guard)*. Asgard was divided into different realms. Odin lived in *Valhalla (val-ha-la)*, a great banquet hall. There was a feast with amazing food and wine every night. Soldiers who died in battle would either go to Valhalla to feast with Odin or to *Fólkvangr (fulk-van-gar)*. Fólkvangr was a heavenly meadow where Freya lived. Anyone who didn't die bravely in battle went to Helheim.

Fun Fact: There were other realms the dead could go, including one overseen by a giantess at the bottom of the ocean. Drowned sailors went there. The Vikings also believed some spirits could become ghosts.

The only way to get to Valhalla or Fólkvangr was an honorable death in battle. This is why the Vikings didn't fear death in battle. That would have made them a terrifying opponent! Once the Vikings reached Valhalla, they spent their days fighting in preparation for *Ragnarök* (doomsday). On that day, they would fight with Odin to save the universe against the giants and other monsters.

Fun Fact: Warriors who bravely died in battle were called Einherjar (eyen-her-ya).

When a Viking died in battle, he would be greeted by a *Valkyrie (val-kuh-ree)*, a mythical female warrior. The Vikings believed the Valkyrie decided who went to Valhalla or Fólkvangr. The Valkyrie protected soldiers on the battlefield.

A painting of the Einherjar being served by Valkyries in Valhalla. Odin sits on his throne, flanked by one of his wolves.
https://commons.wikimedia.org/w/index.php?curid=5417783

Chapter 6 Activity

Can you guess which statements are true and which are false?

1. Thor was the king of the gods.

2. Odin's horse had eight legs.

3. Loki was the god of light.

4. Balder's only weakness was Loki.

5. The gods lived in Asgard.

6. Helheim was the underworld ruled by the goddess Hel.

7. Valhalla was the only place where brave warriors went when they died.

8. Freya ruled Fólkvangr, while Odin ruled Valhalla.

9. Two cats pulled Thor's chariot.

10. Frey was Freya's twin brother.

Bonus Activity: Have a go at drawing the gods and their animal sidekicks!

Chapter 6 Answers

True or false?

1. Thor was the king of the gods. **False. His father, Odin, was. Thor was the god of thunder and lightning. He was the strongest god.**

2. Odin's horse had eight legs. **True. It was called Sleipnir. Can you remember the other animals Odin had?**

3. Loki was the god of light. **False. Loki was the god of mischief.**

4. Balder's only weakness was Loki. **False. His only weakness was mistletoe.**

5. The gods lived in Asgard. **True.**

6. Helheim was the underworld ruled by the goddess Hel. **True. Can you remember the name of her guard dog?**

7. Valhalla was the only place where brave warriors went when they died. **False. Warriors would either go to Valhalla or Fólkvangr.**

8. Freya ruled Fólkvangr, while Odin ruled Valhalla. **True.**

9. Two cats pulled Thor's chariot. **False. Freya's chariot was pulled by two cats. Thor's chariot was pulled by two goats.**

10. Frey was Freya's twin brother. **True.**

Chapter 7: Tales of Norse Mythology

We've mentioned how the Vikings loved to tell epic sagas about the gods, heroes, and everyday people. Are you ready to hear some of those tales?

The Creation of the World

Before the world was created, there was just a cold, dark, empty void of nothingness called *Ginnungagap (gi-nun-ga-gap)*. Two realms appeared on either side of Ginnungagap. To the north, there was *Niflheim (nih-vl-haym)*, a dark place made only of ice. To the south, *Muspelheim (mus-pel-haym)* formed. Muspelheim was the realm of fire and lava.

When the air from the two realms met, the fire melted the ice. This created the first giant, *Ymir (ee-mer)*. More giants were born, including a giant cow. The cow licked a block of ice. The first god, *Buri (bu-ree)*, came from the ice. Buri's son and his wife would have three sons: Odin, *Ve (vee)*, and *Vili (vi-ley)*.

Ymir kept making more giants. Odin and his brothers did not like that there were more giants than gods. So, they decided to kill Ymir in his sleep. Odin and his brothers created the world from Ymir's remains. His blood became the lakes, rivers, and oceans. His body became the land. Ymir's bones were made into mountains. His teeth became rocks. His hair became the grass and trees. The brothers threw his head into the air. His skull became the sky, and his brain became the clouds. The gods took some fire from Muspelheim to make the stars.

Fun Fact: The Sun and Moon were the beautiful children of an arrogant man. The Sun and Moon were chased by two hungry wolves as they crossed the sky. Ragnarök would start soon after the wolves caught up to the Sun and Moon.

The first humans were made by Odin and his brothers. Men were made from an ash tree. Women were shaped from an elm tree. Odin gave the logs life. Vi made them move and gave them intelligent minds. Vili gave them their shape, senses, feelings, and speech. It was decided that humans would live on earth, which was known as *Midgard*.

Odin

Odin's Eye

We bet you're wondering how such a powerful god like Odin could have lost an eye. Well, it turns out he did it to himself! According to legend, Odin plucked out his eye in exchange for divine wisdom. To get this, he had to drink from a well that was guarded by the wisest god, *Mimir (me-me-uh)*. When Odin drank from the well, he knew everything that had ever happened and would ever happen. He vowed to protect humans and never let evil triumph in the world.

Thor and the Wedding

One night, while Thor was sleeping, a giant crept into his room and stole his hammer. Thor was so angry when he awoke that he caused a terrible storm. He realized he needed a cunning plan to get his hammer back. He knew the best person to ask was Loki.

Loki believed the giants had taken Mjölnir since it killed so many of them. Loki borrowed Freya's feathered cloak and flew to speak with the king of the giants, *Thrym (thrim)*. Thrym told Loki that Mjölnir was hidden underground. He said he would return the hammer if Freya married him. Freya refused.

The gods suggested that Thor should dress up as Freya to trick the giant king. Thor did not like the idea. He was afraid of looking silly. Loki promised to dress as his bridesmaid, so Thor agreed.

Once they were ready, the gods set off in their disguises to the giant's kingdom. Thrym held a huge feast. He was shocked by his bride's appearance and how much she ate! The cunning Loki convinced Thrym that it was nerves. When Thrym placed Mjölnir on his bride's lap, Thor tore off his disguise. He killed Thrym and every other giant there.

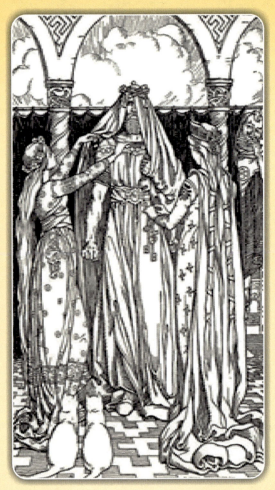

The god Thor is dressed as the goddess Freya. Loki laughs in the background. Freya's two cats watch.
https://commons.wikimedia.org/w/index.php?curid=4597828

Thor Goes Fishing!

In another tale, Thor goes on a fishing trip, but he catches more than just fish! He manages to catch *Jörmungandr (your-moon-gahn-dr)*, a giant sea snake that wraps itself around Midgard. Just as Thor was about to kill the snake with his hammer, his fishing companion cut the line. The serpent swam away.

Fun Fact: Jörmungandr was one of Loki's children.

Sigurd and the Dragon

Sigurd (sig-uhd) wasn't a god. He was a prince. Sigurd had a tutor named *Regin (rey-gin)*, who trained him to be king. One day, Regin told the prince to kill a dragon and take its treasure. Regin explained that the dragon used to be the prince's brother. The brother, *Fafnir (faf-neeuh)*, killed his father for the gold. But the gold was cursed. It would lead to doom for the owner. Fafnir decided to become a dragon to protect it.

Sigurd had to be careful how he approached the dragon since its breath was poisonous. Sigurd decided to dig a hole and hide inside. When the dragon walked over him, he could stab it in its belly and pierce its heart. This plan was very dangerous. The dragon could just as easily trample him or sit on him! Luckily, Sigurd's plan worked.

A drawing of Sigurd tasting the dragon blood.
https://commons.wikimedia.org/wiki/File:Ring45.jpg

Regin told Sigurd to roast the dragon's heart over a fire. Sigurd accidentally burned his finger. He put his finger in his mouth to cool, but there was dragon blood on it. The dragon blood was magical. All of a sudden, Sigurd could hear the birds talking about Regin's evil plan. Regin wanted to eat the dragon's heart because it would give him great wisdom. Then he planned to kill Sigurd and take the gold. Sigurd became blind with rage. He chopped off Regin's head.

Fenrir and Tyr

Loki was the father of Hel, the goddess of Helheim. He was also the father of Jörmungandr, the sea snake. And he also fathered *Fenrir (fen-rer)*, a giant wolf. Fenrir was a major threat to the gods. It was known he would kill Odin during Ragnarök. So, the gods decided to chain the wolf so he couldn't escape. Fenrir kept getting bigger. He kept escaping his bonds.

One day, the gods asked the dwarves to make a magical thread to bind Fenrir. Then the gods challenged Fenrir to test his strength against it. They promised to free him if he couldn't escape. Although the thread looked very weak, Fenrir was not so easily tricked. He said he would only put it on if one of the gods put their hand inside his mouth. The god *Tyr (teer)* bravely volunteered. He was willing to sacrifice his hand for everyone else's safety.

When Fenrir realized he'd been tricked, he bit off Tyr's hand. The gods did not let Fenrir go. He was finally trapped.

Fun Fact: The evil werewolf in the Harry Potter series, Fenrir Greyback, was named after Fenrir.

Fenrir and Tyr.
https://commons.wikimedia.org/w/index.php?curid=106108

Ragnarök

Ragnarök was a series of predicted events that led to the end of the world. During Ragnarök, the gods and men would fight against monsters and giants. First, there would be three terrible winters where men turned against each other. Then another three winters would follow with no summers.

The wolves chasing the Moon and Sun would finally catch up and swallow them. The mountains and trees would fall, freeing the monsters. Fenrir would destroy the earth with fire. The sea snake, Jörmungandr, would rise, poisoning the oceans and sky. A ghost boat carrying frost giants would appear from the sea, and the sky would open up with fire giants. The giants would travel over the *Bifrost* (the rainbow bridge that connects Midgard to Asgard).

Odin would lead the souls of the dead Vikings into battle. Odin would be eaten whole by Fenrir. Thor would be poisoned by Jörmungandr but not before dealing a deadly blow to the snake with his hammer. All of the monsters, giants, and men would die. Most of the gods would die as well. But a new world without evil would emerge. The humans would also be reborn.

A drawing of the battle during Ragnarök.
https://commons.wikimedia.org/w/index.php?curid=1393337

Chapter 7 Activity

Write your own epic story about the Norse gods, heroes, and monsters! Or draw a picture of one of the stories you've read in this chapter.

Chapter 8: Runes and Rituals

Runes

Runes were a type of symbol that made up the Norse alphabet. It was the earliest form of the Germanic language. Runes were carved into wood or stone. They are fairly simple looking and made up of straight lines. The full set of runes used by the Vikings was called *Elder Futhark (foo-thark)*. It had twenty-four runes.

Each rune had a meaning. The runes were split into three groups of eight. The first was ruled by the goddess Freya. The second set was ruled by the god and goddess *Heimdall (hiym-dal)* and *Mordgud (mord-good)*. Heimdall was the guardian of the Bifrost. Mordgud was the guardian of Helheim. The final set of runes was ruled by two other gods, *Tiwaz (tee-vas)* and *Zisa (zee-suh)*.

The *Younger Futhark* had nineteen runes. It began to be used around 800 CE during the Viking Age.

The Vikings believed the runes were made by Odin. In reality, they were created by people who lived in what is now Germany. They then brought the runes to Denmark in 100 CE.

Runes were said to have magical powers. If they were used incorrectly, they could cause someone harm. The Vikings had runemasters who could correctly write them. The Vikings also used runes to tell the future! They would carve runes onto small stones and shake them in a bag. The stones that fell out would tell the future.

Runes weren't just used for their magic. They were also practical. By writing a rune on something, you could claim ownership of it. It is a bit like how we write our names on our clothing or school bags. Runes were used on tombstones and for celebrations. Merchants used them to keep track of sales.

A manuscript from c. 1300 containing one of the oldest and best-preserved texts of the Scanian law. It is written entirely in runes.
https://commons.wikimedia.org/w/index.php?curid=2794167

RITUALS

Weddings

Just like us, the Vikings had weddings. But theirs were a little different. Before the wedding, the groom had to find a sword that belonged to one of his ancestors. He could do this by breaking into a grave or asking a living relative. He would carry the sword to the wedding. He also might carry a hammer to honor Thor.

After honoring the gods, the ceremony would begin. The groom gave the sword to his bride. One day, she would give it to their son. She gave her husband a new sword. Like we do today, they exchanged rings and vows.

Afterward, there was a great feast. The groom plunged his new sword into a pillar. The deeper it went, the luckier their children would be.

Babies

A baby was not considered a person until certain rituals were performed. First, they would be placed on the ground until their father picked them up. By doing this, the father accepted the baby as being his. Then the dad would inspect the baby for any problems. If it had any, it might be left outside to die.

Healthy babies had water sprinkled over them in a ceremony. After this, they had a naming ceremony. The baby then received gifts. It was considered murder to abandon them after the rituals had been completed.

Sacrifices

The Vikings practiced sacrifices to the gods. Usually, these were in the form of *blot sacrifice* (blood sacrifice). These sacrifices happened four times a year. The chief led the blot ceremony. Animals were sacrificed in honor of the gods and then eaten in a feast. The Vikings even sacrificed humans! Human sacrifices were rare.

Funerals

The Vikings laid their dead to rest in several ways. The main two were burial and cremation. Cremations usually took place on a funeral pyre. The ashes were buried. The most important people (such as a chief) were buried or cremated in a ship. This was not a common burial method since it was very expensive. The chief was buried with food, drink, jewels, and weapons. Slaves might be sacrificed as well.

A painting of a Viking funeral where a ship is set on fire at sea.
https://commons.wikimedia.org/w/index.php?curid=78149883

Yule

This winter celebration helped shape modern-day Christmas! Yule celebrates the winter solstice. The solstice takes place twice a year in winter and summer. The winter solstice is when the sun is at its highest point away from the earth. The summer solstice is when the sun is at its closest point.

Much like Christmas today, Yule involved lots of drinking, eating, and playing games. The Vikings made a large wheel that represented the sun. They set it on fire and rolled it down a hill to encourage the sun's return. They decorated yule logs and evergreen trees. Children wore goat skins in honor of Thor's goats.

Chapter 8 Activity

1. How many runes were in the Elder Futhark?

2. What magical properties did the Vikings believe runes had?

3. What did the couple swap in their wedding ceremonies?

4. What did Yule celebrate?

5. Why were only important people buried or cremated in a boat?

Chapter 8 Answers

1. How many runes were in the Elder Futhark Runes? Twenty-four.

2. What magical properties did the Vikings believe runes had? They could predict the future.

3. What did the couple swap in their wedding ceremonies? Swords and rings.

4. What did Yule celebrate? The winter solstice.

5. Why were only important people buried or cremated in a boat? Because it was very expensive.

Chapter 9: What Happened to the Vikings?

Generally, the end of the Viking Age is considered to be 1066 CE. This was the year when the King Harald Hardrada of Norway was killed at the *Battle of Stamford Bridge*. The battle is an easy way to bookmark the Viking Age. However, the Vikings weren't all killed in the battle.

An image of the Battle of Stamford Bridge.
https://commons.wikimedia.org/wiki/File:Battle_of_Stamford_Bridge_full.png

As you now know, Vikings weren't just raiders. They were farmers, merchants, and fishermen. At the end of the Viking Age, the Vikings didn't disappear or die. They went back to their normal lives and stopped raiding. But why did they stop?

Because of the changes in Europe, raiding became less profitable. At the start of the Viking Age, many Vikings were landowning farmers. They could afford a ship and crew. But by the end of the Viking Age, the majority of land and wealth belonged to only a few families. The rest of society had to stay and work to pay for rent and to feed their families. They didn't have the time or money to go on raids.

Raiding also became more difficult. Countries were better prepared to handle raids. By the end of the Viking Age, many countries had well-trained and well-armed soldiers. They were not afraid of the Vikings. They also wouldn't fall for the Vikings' usual tactics. The Vikings were unorganized. They found these new armies far more difficult to defeat.

Monasteries built towers that were easily defendable. Monks moved at the first sign of trouble, taking their valuables with them. Some monasteries chose to move farther inland.

The Middleton Cross, a Christian cross showing a Viking in armor.
Amanda Slater from Coventry, West Midlands, UK,
CC BY-SA 2.0 <https://creativecommons.org/licenses/by-sa/2.0>,
via Wikimedia Commons, https://commons.wikimedia.org/w/index.php?curid=89376572

Another reason the Vikings stopped raiding was due to their conversion to Christianity. As the Vikings began to settle in Christian countries, they started to adopt the religion. In the beginning, the Vikings worshiped the Old Norse gods alongside the Christian God. Over time, they became fully Christian. The Vikings also adopted other aspects from European countries, such as writing, laws, and culture.

So, the Vikings didn't disappear or die out. Instead, they stopped raiding. They began changing their beliefs and customs. People no longer referred to them as a collective group of Vikings. Instead, they began referring to them as being from their individual countries.

Chapter 9 Activity

Can you fill in the blanks?

The Viking Age ended for many reasons. The end of the Viking Age took place in _____ CE with the death of King Harald of _____. However, many factors contributed to its end. First, Vikings no longer went on _____. They didn't have the time or money to do so. Also, raiding became harder. Monasteries built _____ to defend themselves. The _____ were also better prepared, armed, and trained. Finally, the Vikings converted to _____ and adopted European customs, including _____, laws, and culture.

Chapter 9 Answers

The Viking Age ended for many reasons. The end of the Viking Age took place in **1066** CE with the death of King Harald of **Norway**. However, many factors contributed to its end. First, Vikings no longer went on **raids**. They didn't have the time or money to do so. Also, raiding became harder. Monasteries built **towers** to defend themselves. The **armies** were also better prepared, armed, and trained. Finally, the Vikings converted to **Christianity** and adopted European customs, including **writing**, laws, and culture.

Chapter 10: 10 Fun Viking Facts

1. Vikings didn't wear horned helmets.

Most Viking Halloween costumes or depictions of Vikings in movies and TV show Vikings wearing a helmet with two horns. However, there's no evidence to suggest they did. It wasn't until the 19th century that they were painted wearing them. In fact, the Vikings may not have even worn helmets at all! Only one complete Viking helmet has ever been found. It's likely Vikings fought without a helmet or used a leather head covering.

The Gjermundbu helmet found in Norway. It belonged to an equestrian warrior, perhaps a very rich and powerful chieftain. The helmet was made between 950 and 1000. It was destroyed, possibly ritually, before or during the funeral.

Wolfmann, CC BY-SA 4.0 <https://creativecommons.org/licenses/by-sa/4.0>, via Wikimedia Commons, https://commons.wikimedia.org/w/index.php?curid=112456796

2. **Viking gentlemen preferred being blond.**

   Viking men who weren't blessed with naturally blond hair used a soap containing lots of lye to lighten their hair. The soap also treated head lice too!

3. **All of the days of the week (apart from Saturday) in English are named after Viking gods.**

4. Sunday is for the god of the sun, *Sol*. Monday is for the goddess of the moon, *Mani*. Tuesday is Tyr's day. Wednesday is for Odin. It started as Wodin's day (Odin is sometimes called Wodin). Thursday is Thor's day. Friday is Frigg's day. Saturday came from the Roman god *Saturn*.

   We can thank the Vikings for more than just the days of the week. At least 139 words in the English language come from Old Norse!

5. **Vikings were feminists.**

   Okay, they weren't feminists in the way we know today. But Viking women had more rights than many other women in Europe at that time. Viking women could own property, get divorced, and even get their *dowry* back. (A dowry was money paid by the bride's family to the groom.) Viking women also held important positions. They could be priestesses, oracles, or poets. Women even fought in battle as shieldmaidens.

Norwegian nationalistic postcard showing a shieldmaiden drawn by Andreas Bloch.
https://commons.wikimedia.org/w/index.php?curid=2454434

6. The word "berserk" comes from the Vikings.

Some Vikings believed they would become wolves or bears when fighting. They would go to battle wearing only animal skins. They carried no weapons. Instead, they used their bare hands and teeth to fight. Before the fight, they lived in the wild as their chosen animal.

The bear men were Berserkers (bear-shirts). They would literally go berserk (out of control with anger or excitement) while fighting.

7. Vikings dyed their teeth red.

Archaeologists have discovered the remains of Vikings with horizontal lines carved into their top front row of teeth. It is thought these grooves were filled with red dye. This likely terrified their opponents in battle since it would have looked like blood. It sure sounds scary, especially if they were a berserker too!

8. Vikings enjoyed skiing!

Skis were invented approximately six thousand years ago in Scandinavia. It is possible skis were invented even earlier in Russia or China. During the Viking Age, skis were seen as a convenient way to get around in the snow. The Vikings skied for fun. The Vikings loved skiing so much that they even had a god for it!

9. The Vikings skipped lunch.

Today, it's common to have three meals a day with snacks in between. But the Vikings only had two meals. Breakfast (*dagmal*) was served an hour or two after waking up. Breakfast was usually leftovers from the night before or porridge. *Nattmal* was served at the end of the day after work.

Vikings were fond of fish, but they also ate stew, meat, bread, and fruit. They washed their food down with a jug of mead (an alcoholic drink made from honey). While their meals sound quite tasty, I'm not sure if I could go without my lunch! Could you?

10. Vikings were a hit with the ladies!

The Anglo-Saxons were jealous of the well-groomed Vikings because they were more attractive to women! One scholar said they "made themselves too acceptable to English women by their elegant manners and their care of their person. They combed their hair every day, bathed every Saturday, and even changed their garments often."

11. Vikings believed in zombies!

The Vikings believed in two different types of zombies. If proper precautions weren't taken before burial, a person could become a *draugr (druy-ghur)* or *haugbui (haug-bee)*. Haugbui were reasonably harmless. They stayed buried. But draugrs would rise out of their grave to harm the living.

A Viking burial ground in Lindholm Høje, Denmark.
https://commons.wikimedia.org/w/index.php?curid=2930078

Chapter 10 Activity

Here are some fun Viking pictures to color in!

https://pixabay.com/vectors/vikings-ship-sailing-ship-boat-293960/

https://pixabay.com/illustrations/man-viking-barbarian-ax-soldier-1706964/

If you want to learn more about tons of other exciting historical periods, check out our other books!

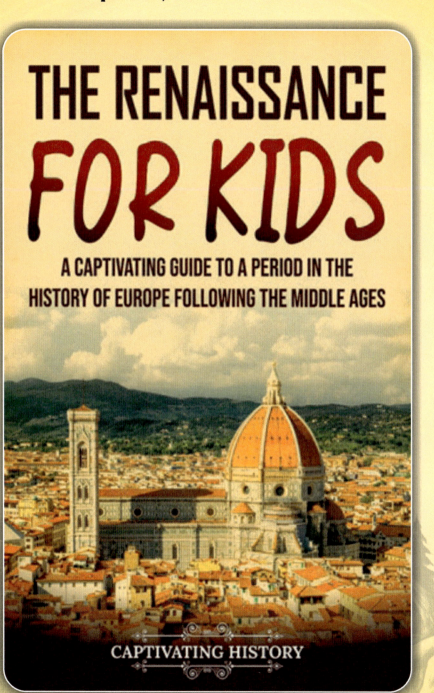

We hope you enjoyed this book. If you did any of the fun activities at the end of the chapters, we would love to see your work! Ask a parent or guardian to help you post your art. Or have them help you email it to us directly!

Facebook: https://www.facebook.com/captivatinghistory

Instagram: @captivatinghistorybooks

Email: matt@captivatinghistory.com

Bibliography

If you enjoyed this book and want to learn more about the Vikings, here are some suggestions for fun and educational books, YouTube videos, and websites!

Books

A list of great books can be found here: https://www.theschoolrun.com/best-childrens-books-about-vikings.

Alexander, Heather. *A Child's Introduction to Norse Mythology: Odin, Thor, Loki, and Other Viking Gods, Goddesses, Giants, and Monsters (A Child's Introduction Series)*. 2018.

Deary, Terry. *The Vicious Vikings*. 1998.

Higgins, Nadia. *National Geographic Kids Everything Vikings: All the Incredible Facts and Fierce Fun You Can Plunder*. 2015.

Morpurgo, Michael. *Beowulf*. 2015. (Although this is technically an adaption of an Anglo-Saxon saga, it involves a Scandinavian warrior.)

YouTube

An Incredible Viking Voyage—Made Entirely of Paper, National Geographic. https://www.youtube.com/watch?v=eGLu2Frqwis

Learning Made Fun. https://www.youtube.com/c/MrBradleyLearningMadeFun

TED-Ed. https://www.youtube.com/teded

Horrible Histories. https://www.youtube.com/c/HorribleHistoriesOfficial

Websites

https://vikings.mrdonn.org/stories.html

https://www.bbc.co.uk/programmes/articles/20stJyBvh9mv7kpSVgDfKPw/viking-sagas-age-7-11

https://kids.nationalgeographic.com/

https://www.storynory.com/

Made in the USA
Coppell, TX
10 February 2025